Volume 7 Issue 1
The Wholeness and Harmony Issue
www.inspiritmagazine.com

Editor's Note

The power is within you to create a sense of Wholeness and Harmony in your life.

Yet for a lot of us, we often get stuck on the treadmill of peace and connection being an ever elusive feeling as we go about life and all that it entails for us. In this issue we have combined our efforts to share some of how Wholeness and Harmony works in each of our lives, while graciously sharing the information we believe can help achieve more Wholeness and Harmony in your life.

You'll find contributions profiling Yoga, Buddhism and a powerful article from Nicola McIntosh on the Tree of Life, while Laura Naomi's offering with Shamanism and the balance of Nature is sure to inspire.

We are blessed to feature world renowned Parapsychologist Dr. Ciaran O'Keeffe from the UK's "Most Haunted" TV show, who thanks to Danni from Ghost of Oz, shares his thoughts on how Science is increasingly meeting Spirituality.

This issue we say goodbye to Billie Dean. This is Billie's last contribution and we thank her for all her Animal Wisdom over the last twelve months and send our ongoing support for Billie's animal conservation work. Thank you Billie, we will miss you.

This issue we also welcome on board Amanda Coppa from Cosmic Codes who'll be offering some of her inSightful Moon Magic with each issue, and we also welcome Therese Chesworth back to the team to assist with editing. Welcome ladies!

And before I close out this issue of Editor's note, I wish to thank Nicola McIntosh for all the stunning graphic design work she has so willingly contributed to inSpirit Magazine over the last twelve months. You've taken a dream and made it more beautiful than we could imagine and as your designing goes in new directions, I and the inSpirit team thank you.

With love & gratitude, *Kerrie*

In This Issue

14 Centered in Oneness

- 3   Yoga: The Doorway to Spirit
- 4   Inside a Doctor's Paranormal Mind: Dr Ciaran O'Keeffe
- 6   Planetary Wholeness and Harmony and your Diet
- 8   Wholeness and Harmony
- 10   The Tree of Life
- 12   The Power of a Name
- 13   What is Buddhism
- 16   Shell Healing for Health, Happiness and Harmony
- 17   Everyday Enchantment with the Elements
- 18   Living with Spirit
- 21   Gift of being a Sensitive
- 22   Finding Wholeness and Harmony with Animals and Nature
- 23   Chalk and Cheese
- 25   How to Relieve Stress and Get Back Your Flow

Regular Columns

- 11   Goddess inSpiration
- 13   Cosmic Codes
- 20   For the Love of Angels
- 25   inSpirit Reviews
- 26   inSpirit Directory

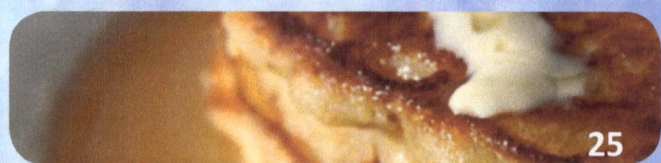
25

13

4

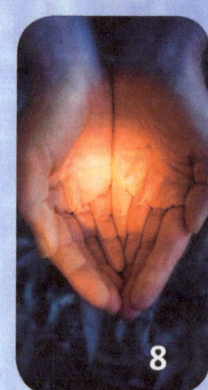
8

THE TEAM

MANAGING EDITOR Kerrie Wearing

CREATIVE TEAM Kerrie Wearing, Nicolle Poll, Alex Cayas, Therese Chesworth

EDITOR Nicolle Poll, Therese Chesworth

REGULAR CONTRIBUTORS Kerrie Wearing, Nicolle Poll, Nicola McIntosh, Susanne Hartas, Billie Dean, Brendan D. Murphy, Gem~mer, Meadow Linn, Alex Cayas, Natasha Heard, Laura Naomi, Kye Crow, Reilly McCarron, Rita Maher, Amanda Coppa

GUEST CONTRIBUTORS Danni Stark, Lucy Proud, Nicole Humber

GRAPHIC DESIGN Kerrie Wearing, Nicola McIntosh

COVER ARTWORK Nicolle Poll

Produced by Kerrie Wearing and inSpirit Publishing, inSpirit Magazine is designed to provide a respectful forum for like-minded souls to share in a community which aims to provide informative views, opinions and education regarding the experience of living with Spirit. Disclaimer: While every care has been taken to provide the reader with accurate, inSpiring and thought-provoking information, the Publishers take no responsibility for the accuracy of information and views expressed by the Contributors. The views and opinions expressed by contributors are not necessarily shared by the Editor Publishers.

YOGA:
The Doorway to Spirit

by Lucy Proud

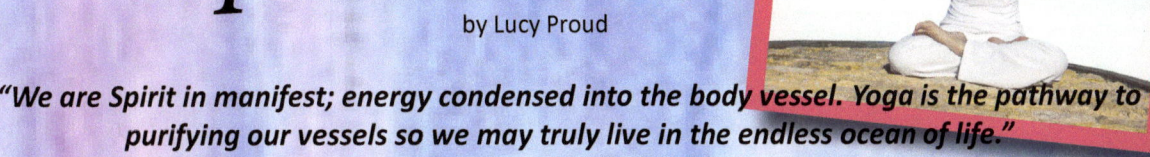

"We are Spirit in manifest; energy condensed into the body vessel. Yoga is the pathway to purifying our vessels so we may truly live in the endless ocean of life."

The word Yoga itself means "union." It is a system seemingly deriving from India and the Himalayas more than 2500 years ago, that aims to unify the multi-dimensional nature of the human being with the Universal Consciousness or Spirit.

The asanas, or postures, that have gained widespread popularity in recent decades are only one aspect of this profound practice, or way of life to unfolding the infinite nature. It is said in the Bible: "Be still and know that I am God." In these few words lies the key to the science of Yoga. This ancient spiritual science offers a direct means of stilling the natural turbulence of thoughts, emotions and restlessness of body that prevent us from knowing what and who we really are; our true (Buddha) nature.

Why all the fuss about mind? Suffering exists when we look outside of ourselves for fulfillment. We are living in a world that conditions us to believe that outer attainments can give us what we want. We are caught up in doing rather than being, in action rather than awareness. By the practice of Yoga we can cultivate presence. There is a beautiful and simple saying - "Wherever the mind goes is where energy flows." Ordinarily our awareness and energies are directed outward, to the things of this world. Yoga is a simple process of reversing the ordinary outward flow of energy and consciousness so that the mind and life-force (prana) is directed inwardly to purify, regenerate and transform our limited awareness into actually experiencing peace and truth. Within the mind is always movement and beyond the mind there is always feeling. We are like the infinite ocean with endless waves of constant thought and emotion. If our mind is restless and agitated, the waves (the thoughts and emotions) become unsettled, rough and wild, yet if our mind is at peace each wave becomes more like the ocean of peace.

Hatha Yoga, the system of physical postures, or asanas, whose higher purpose is to purify the body are the keys that can unlock the doors to this inner peace and the awakened self. Like any discipline it can take time and effort to develop the strength and flexibility required for advanced postures but if you try to only perfect the pose you will miss the magic. Attention must be drawn deeper to the inner self and the in-breath will take you there. I like to view my practice of Yoga as a moving meditation, a sensory journey towards discovering peace within the ebb and flow of life. Even within the stillness of the body and the spaces between thought there is always constant flow, because the nature of energy is infinite. When we practice moving in flow, we cultivate prana, which can then clear stagnation and blockages in the body, and create more balance. As we learn to become at one with flow of breath and body, life and prana flows from within us, not just around us. When we access this creative intelligence from within, life becomes and awakened experience of being, not doing.

Why practice Yoga? How does living with less stress, more peace and happiness sound? Yoga gifts us tools to become our own healers and directors of our life. Not to say that life's challenges completely disappear but the more we practice Yoga authentically, the more we become equipped to meeting life's demands from a place of peace. The practice of Yoga creates a foundational structure from which we can stand upon our own altar of strength, wisdom, truth and love. Above and beyond Yoga makes us feel good! And as the law of karma states what we feel, think, do and radiate is what naturally comes back to us.

The breath is the direct link to our spiritual and physical energies in union. This is what is meant by living in the heart. When we live from the heart, in a state of feeling as opposed to thinking, we are more aligned with our intuition and truths.

Yoga is a way of life. By working from within, Yoga helps peel away the layers of resistance that prevent us from living life fully awake, present, balanced and in harmony. To live in union with ourselves, others and the Divine Universe is to live in the ultimate state of bliss.

Namaste and divine shanti (peace) blessings.

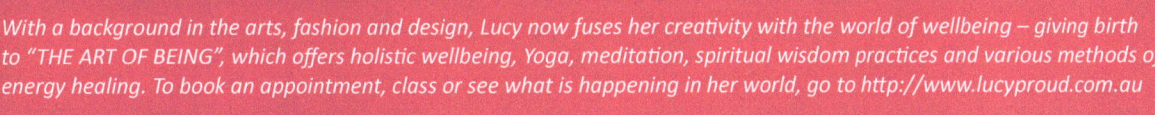

With a background in the arts, fashion and design, Lucy now fuses her creativity with the world of wellbeing – giving birth to "THE ART OF BEING", which offers holistic wellbeing, Yoga, meditation, spiritual wisdom practices and various methods of energy healing. To book an appointment, class or see what is happening in her world, go to http://www.lucyproud.com.au

Inside a Doctors Paranormal Mind

WORLD RENOWNED PARAPSYCHOLOGIST AND FORENSIC PSYCHOLOGIST DR. CIARAN O'KEEFFE TALKS WITH DANNI REMAILI FROM GHOSTS OF OZ ON ALL THINGS SCIENCE, THE BRAIN AND THE PARANORMAL.

A fine Sydney evening finds Dr. Ciaran O'Keeffe in his office on a dreary English morning on the other side of the world. However, nothing could stop me and the highly acclaimed academic and parapsychologist from sharing a few jokes and laughter before we ventured into the world of fringe science and the paranormal. Dr. Ciaran James O'Keeffe is an English born Psychologist with years of academic and experiential research into Psychology as a science, and the paranormal as a fringe science. Armed with the power of research and knowledge, Ciaran O'Keeffe opens up to me about the wonders of the paranormal, the dangers of public scrutiny and what it means to be a part of the parapsychology phenomena.

Danni Remaili: Let's first just wrap our heads around the idea of Parapsychology, especially for those new to the field. Are we talking just pure clairvoyance or is there a science to this?

Ciaran O'Keeffe: Well, Parapsychology is the scientific study of human experiences, but outside what we know of conventional science. If you then break it down into its categories, Parapsychology is scientific study of three areas - ESP, PK and also Survival or After Death Communication. ESP is an umbrella term that refers to clairvoyance, precognition and telepathy; so any sort of mind to mind communication, as it were. PK is Psycho-Kinesis; the kind of 'spoon bending' idea, and then Survival, the third category which actually is the least researched in Parapsychology to be honest. It's any form of evidence or experiences that give a hint that we survive after death. So it can be haunting experiences, or poltergeist experiences, but it can also be Mediumship communication, anything like that. That's Parapsychology in a nutshell.

DR: It's quite a broad subject, isn't it?

CO: Most definitely!

DR: Now, we've seen you on Famous and Frightened at Chillingham Castle in England (one of my personal favourites), and we've also seen you in many episodes on Jane Goldman Investigates, however most famously you made an appearance on Most Haunted. How have these experiences influenced your life and your research? Has anything changed because of these experiences?

CO: Well…..I'm talking to you. (Laughs)

DR: (Laughs)

CO: That's a big change! I'm talking to you - Ghosts of Oz. Being involved in Paracon Australia - that's a huge change. Being a part of TV Programs has been phenomenal in terms of exposure; in terms of people hearing about my research. Because of that I get to talk to people I wouldn't normally talk to, because they hear about my work. If anything, these sorts of programs have given the motivation and the impetus for the field to ride in. It just means that parapsychologists now are able to talk to ghost busters and ghost investigators. If anything, the big benefit is that the field has widened. There's loads more communication from me to others, and from others to me, which I think is brilliant. The problem could've been - I mean I've always been involved in ghost investigations, but prior to being involved in those shows, I was a Parapsychologist and Investigative Psychologist in a University; in a Laboratory.

DR: All tucked away.

CO: All tucked away, yes, (laughs) in my ivory tower, with my lab coat and stethoscope. Nobody would've known about my stuff, you know. As a parapsychologist I published papers on these sorts of things, but generally the public don't hear about this stuff unless they've subscribed. So TV has given an impetus for people to learn about Parapsychology. Of course the great thing is, accessing these great locations. You mentioned Chillingham Castle. I doubt whether, as an academic, I'd have that type of access to that location. Meeting the people that I've met. Jane Goldman, for example, an amazing person who actually is known for her work writing about the X Files. Since then she's become the script writer for The Woman in Black, Stardust and the latest X-Men films. It's been fantastic speaking to her about all things Paranormal and Parapsychology.

DR: For someone with a strong academic background, someone who values education, it's quite disappointing to see that the study of Parapsychology is still being criticised and ostracised by many academics and non-academics. Why do you think this is so?

CO: Mainstream science certainly has a view of Parapsychology that 'it shouldn't be studied' because it's apparently a field that's rife with fraud - people hallucinating and making things up. They are basically seeing Parapsychology as not a science, and there are two rebuttals to that. Parapsychology is a science, by the definition of the word Science. It uses scientific methods to investigate these experiences. A majority of it happens in a lab and there are very few Parapsychologists that get to go out into the field, and I pride myself on being one of them. But Parapsychology is viewed quite negatively, I think because of its history. Because there have been lots of people caught making things up, lots of frauds, and psychics caught using trickery. Science turns a blind eye, and it's very worrying too. I don't want to get heavy and on my soapbox, but the fact that so many people believe in this sort of stuff; in ghosts, an afterlife, any paranormal experience, I think it's arrogant of Scientists to ignore it! I think they should at least try.

DR: It's quite confusing though, because there are so many funded paranormal TV shows and entertainment, it makes you wonder why the study of Parapsychology is placed on the backburner. Is it because we're lazy, entertainment-hungry human beings, or does it go deeper than that?

CO: (Laughs) Lazy, I love that! I think that's a key part of it - we are entertainment hungry. I think for TV companies, there's a desire to make things entertaining. Certainly when it comes to ghost investigations, that's the prime motivation. You need to grab the audience, have them tuned in for that hour, or whatever length of time it is. They must make it exciting, but the reality of some ghost investigations is that it can be quite mundane and boring. Sometimes things don't happen. Similar to the analogy of watching paint dry. They're not going to sit for an hour doing that. With that pressure, I can understand why they present the ghost investigations the way they do. But in saying that, yes, a lot of these production companies have money behind them to produce these shows. It'd be nice if some of that money (Oh my, sounds like I'm pleading!), it'd be nice if some of that money came toward academia. But it's like a vicious cycle, if there's no money in Parapsychology, academics are not keen on investing their time. And if there aren't any Parapsychologists then it's not considered worthy of investment.

DR: In regards to the investigation, what can you, as Dr. Ciaran O'Keeffe, bring to the table? What's needed? Are there any ideas or concerns that people must take into account when undergoing an experience like the paranormal investigation?

CO: There are lots of things. I love ghost hunting, I've been doing it since I was a teenager. The Parapsychology hat I wear is a scientific one, so I guess for me, I'd be bringing critical thinking and scepticism to the table of any paranormal investigation. I don't mean cynicism; I don't mean being cynical or dismissive, I just mean questioning. Being open-minded about the possibility, but if you hear a noise, you're not immediately thinking it's the four horseman of the apocalypse. You actually investigate it; take a sceptical and critical thinking stance, and you look at the possible alternative explanations. My background is in Investigative Psychology, and part of my training is in interviewing techniques, and there's a lot that we know in Psychology and Investigative Psychology in terms of interviewing and how that can affect what people say in terms of an incident that has happened. We know that from the crime side of things, so why can't we apply that to the ghost investigations? If you've got a case where there are being reports made about a haunting, then you interview them appropriately. Ask them relevant and varied questions because if you don't, you're going to get exaggeration and false information. The last thing I'd bring is ethics, oh, and those flashing gadgets we all like to play with!

DR: Speaking of the challenges we face in the paranormal world, you have a book out called The Paranormal Clash with Billy Roberts. Why do you think there is still this fear of merging the spiritual and scientific world?

CO: I think it's because of the way Science is viewed. Science nowadays is becoming more of a belief system. For example, if you are a Scientist, therefore you can't entertain the idea that there is life after death, because if you do that you're delving into the world of religion and spiritualism. It's just not fair, and I think that's the fundamental issue. In terms of my book, which is a dialogue between myself and Billy Roberts, we have a lot of differing views and sometimes we agree. We're open to dialogue and that's important. As long as you're talking, it's great!

DR: Completely agree with you on that one there. Dr. Ciaran O'Keeffe what's next on the agenda?

CO: At the moment I'm involved with producing my own online series "Ghostlands", and people can find it at youtube.com/ghostlandsonline. This comes about because of being involved with "Most Haunted" and "Famous and Frightened". People have been saying that I should do my own show, and my wife and I have been talking and planning for a number of years. Then it got to this year and we thought "Right, let's do it!" We wanted to make sure we were capturing the investigation so we had enough CCTV footage and camera footage that we could analyse it like any investigation. But also, people can have access to how raw it is and see from my perspective. Of course I'm still doing my school; the School of Parapsychology and I'm also writing a book called "If I Were a Ghost".

Danielle has a strong affiliation to Parapsychology and the impact of the brain on paranormal experiences. She is a Secondary English and Drama Teacher and Co-host/Researcher/Presenter of Ghosts of Oz on Alive90.5fm

PLANETARY WHOLENESS AND HARMONY AND YOUR DIET:

Brendan D. Murphy provides some thought-provoking facts about our reliance on Meat in our diets

We in the West have long been conditioned - starting from when we're too young to know any better - to believe that we need to eat the flesh of (certain) animals to survive, and that we would be nutritionally deficient if we did not. Other animals, of course, are off-limits, or, at the very least, undesirable choices as food for varying reasons. Few of us would willingly kill and eat our beloved household pets, for instance, because we have established emotional connections with them. In contrast, most decent people have become disconnected, through modern living, from sheep, cows, chickens, turkeys, and pigs (to name just a few). Through that disconnection, we have lost our empathy for, and sense of kinship with, these sentient, intelligent creatures. Now, a cow is just a milk machine to be used at our convenience.

Aside from the fact that, for example, beef's protein, is poorly assimilated by the human digestive system (which is that of a herbivore's), and, ignoring the fact that cow's milk (and animal protein in general) is actually leeching calcium from your bones by throwing your acid-based pH system out of balance and into the acidic range (thus laying a foundation for a plethora of health maladies), there are monumental ecological problems that stem from our exploitation of literally billions of innocent animals around the world (particularly cows).

In other words, our dangerous reliance on animal protein in our diets is slowly but surely destroying not just our bones and arteries, but the planet. (It bears mentioning that monoculture agricultural practises in general are causing a lot of damage in their own right - it's not only animal products that are the problem, but they are easily the biggest problem.)

The schisms, fallacies, and blind spots that Carnism ("the invisible belief system, or ideology, that conditions people to eat certain animals"), in particular, rests upon and depends on for its survival as a meme and dogma have created (or perhaps fuelled) a profound disconnect between us and the animals themselves, and - crucially for our survival - between our everyday choices and the real-world human, socioeconomic, and ecological effects (costs) of those choices.

Consider:

The United Nations Food and Agriculture Organization estimates that nearly 870 million people of the 7.1 billion people in the world, or one in eight, were suffering from chronic undernourishment in 2010-2012. Almost all the hungry people, 852 million, live in developing countries, representing 15 percent of the population of developing countries. There are 16 million people undernourished in developed countries.

Now consider the words of animal rights activist and expert Gary Yourofsky: "Every 2-3 seconds a human dies of starvation. But chickens, turkeys, pigs; they never miss a meal. Meat, dairy and egg eating is the worst form of human and animal abuse. And when it comes to pure environmental destruction, air pollution, water pollution, deforestation - nothing competes with animal agriculture."

Each year in America alone, an estimated 9 billion broiler chickens, 113 million pigs, 33 million cows and 250 million turkeys are raised as "food" in "dark, filthy, pestilent barns."

Let's take it one step further, and hear from former cattle rancher turned vegan advocate Howard Lyman: "[M]eat kills. It kills us just as dead as tobacco kills us, but far more frequently. It is far and away the number one cause of death and disease in America." The saturated fat and cholesterol in animal flesh causes heart disease by clogging arteries. Eliminate meat in the diet and replace it with nourishing fruit, veg, and superfoods, and you eliminate a truckload of heart disease.

More than this, the planetary resources that are wasted in the process of fuelling our self-destructive meat-eating ways are truly staggering.

Some statistics from a 1993 Beyond Beef presentation:

A quarter pound of hamburger from South America costs 55 square feet of rain forest. Ninety percent of the surface water in Iowa is contaminated with agricultural chemicals. Half of the antibiotics produced in the United States are used in livestock production. In the last 200 years we have used up 75 percent of our topsoil. It takes 16 pounds of grain to produce one pound of beef.

Even the UN has recommended a shift towards plant-based eating in a 2010 report titled The Environmental Impacts of Consumption and Production, stating that "fossil fuels and agriculture, especially the raising of livestock for meat and dairy products" are having a "disproportionately high impact on people and the planet's life support systems."

The panel found that animals in agribusiness are fed a whopping half of all the world's crops - so that we can then kill and eat the animals! The panel concluded that "a substantial reduction of [environmental] impacts would only be possible with a substantial worldwide diet change, away from animal products."

A UN News Centre Report from 2006 revealed:

Livestock now use 30 per cent of the planet's land surface, mostly permanent pasture but also including 33 per cent of the global arable land used for producing feed for livestock. Massive deforestation is occurring to create new pastures, especially in Latin America where, for example, some 70 per cent of former forests in the Amazon have been turned over to grazing.

Additionally, "Agriculture, particularly meat and dairy products, accounts for 70% of global freshwater consumption, 38% of the total land use and 19% of the world's greenhouse gas emissions, says the report…"

Our blind spots on this issue are slowly but surely creating more and more separation and disharmony, both amongst ourselves as humans, and between us and the environment and the animals we are currently exploiting.

I ask "Are our current agricultural and dietary practises in alignment with our core values as 'spiritual' people?"

www.carnism.org

World Hunger Education Service, 2013 World Hunger and Poverty Facts and Statistics, http://www.worldhunger.org/articles/Learn/world%20hunger%20facts%202002.htm#Number_of_hungry_people_in_the_world

Paul Solotaroff writing for Rolling Stone, In the Belly of the Beast, December 2013.

Howard Lyman, Mad Cowboy, Scribner, 1998, p 23.

Deanna Isaacs, Lecture Notes: Howard Lyman's Case Against Cattle, http://www.chicagoreader.com/chicago/lecture-notes-howard-lymans-case-against-cattle/Content?oid=881627

Tracy H., UN Urges Shift to Plant-Based Diet, http://diggingthroughthedirt.blogspot.com.au/2010/06/un-panel-urges-shift-to-plant-based.html

Felicity Carus, The Guardian, UN urges global move to meat- and dairy-free diet, http://www.theguardian.com/environment/2010/jun/02/un-report-meat-free-diet, June 2010.

Brendan D. Murphy is a researcher, speaker, musician, and the author of The Grand Illusion: A Synthesis of Science and Spirituality – Book 1 (TGI 1), described by author Sol Luckman as a "masterpiece." Brendan is also a certified Psych-K facilitator, a certified DNA Potentiator (Potentiation is the first DNA activation in Luckman's Regenetics Method) and has received formal EFT training (levels 1 and 2). The Grand Illusion—along with free book excerpts and articles—is available at www.brendandmurphy.net.

Maitland Gaol will play host to Australian and International speakers. Which include but are not limited to Dr Ciaran O'Keeffe from the UK television series *Most Haunted* and Ben Hansen former FBI agent and mostly known as a television host and the lead investigator of SyFy channel's *Fact or Faked: Paranormal Files*.

The Two day conference will feature lectures, panels and workshops on a range of topics with everything from Yowies, Triggers in consciousness, Time Travel, Global Crop Circle Phenomenon, Investigative Psychology methods in haunting, The Interplay of Media and Technology on Belief, OUIJASTITIONS – Ouija through the Ages and much more all being explored in this exciting event.

www.paraconaustralia.com

Maitland Gaol - May 10th & 11th 2014

Wholeness and Harmony

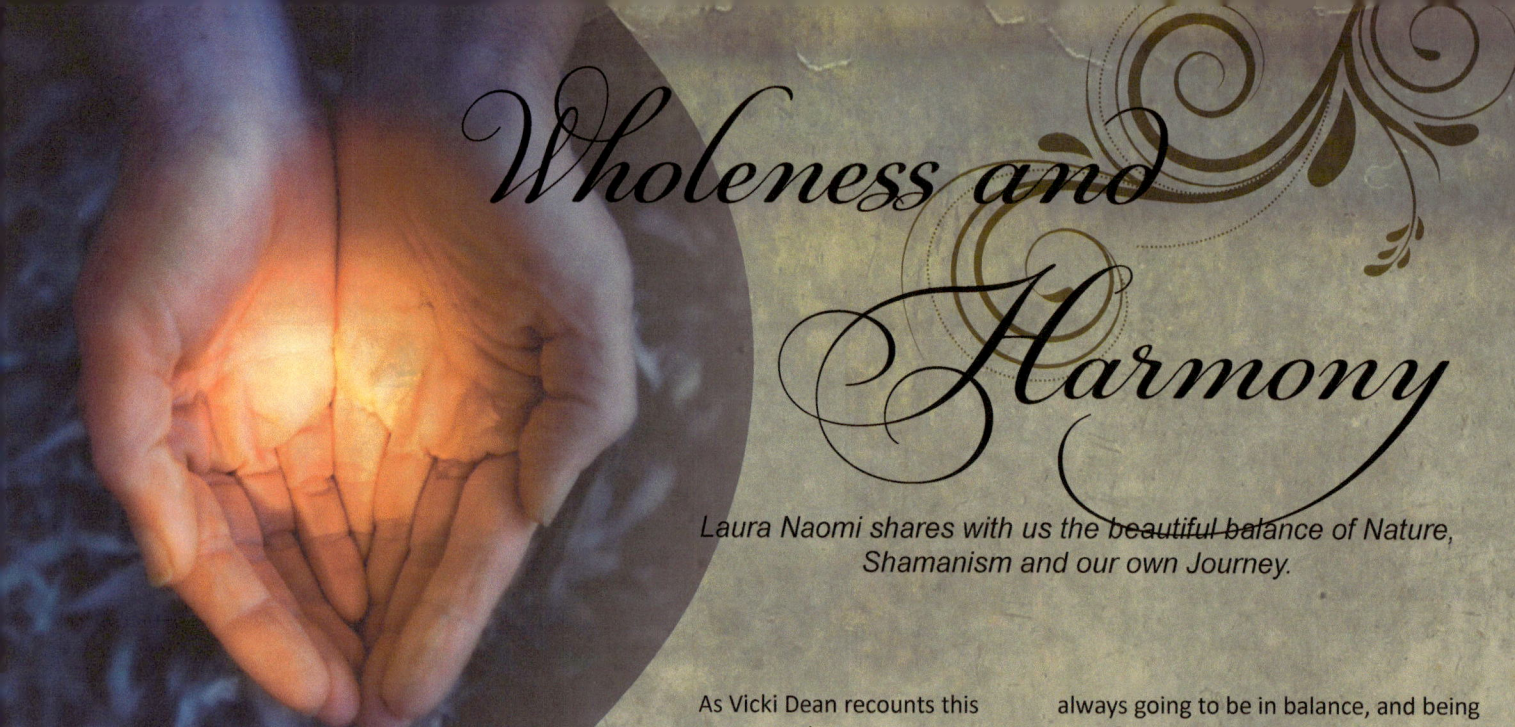

Laura Naomi shares with us the beautiful balance of Nature, Shamanism and our own Journey.

"Yesterday, while I was outside, I heard rustling sounds in the leaves and I looked up to see a rock wallaby with her baby. I was just going about my day when my busyness was, for a minute suspended as I witnessed the baby learning to listen and to forage – a mimic of her mum. In a moment of fear it nuzzled to get back into the pouch, however it's too big. It calls me to the Vision I have for the next stage of my life and its infancy and the need to carefully nourish."

As Vicki Dean recounts this encounter, her energy carries a gentle and vast wisdom. Within this gentleness she holds a space of great nourishment where the environment responds with a quiet pause. Vicki Dean is a senior lecturer and Director of Circalore – Shamanic Studies. For over 30 years she has been involved in Shamanism and creative and healing arts.

An integral facet of Shamanism is about finding the balance of nature within our own nature, and in turn, harmony is offered to us in many forms. Like the seasons of Mother Earth, change is inevitable, and we also share the seasons of life through our wondrous journey of Spirit. Dean tells of her relationship with Shamanism "There is the concept of gratitude and praise and giving thanks. I look to Earth and thank her for holding me and nurturing me. I thank Spirit for this day on Earth. The Shamanic path offers the opportunity to see what is out of balance in myself (or environment) and offers journeys, ceremonies and rituals to learn and regain harmony."

When I ask her about how prominent Mother Earth has been in her journey, she responds "Nature is my greatest teacher." Although we are not always going to be in balance, and being out of harmony allows us to return to awareness as there is always something to experience or learn. In the world the way it is, it can sometimes be easy to get caught up in unbalanced and fragmented energy - it reflects the energy of humanity on a larger scale that rests in our inner chambers for greater consciousness and understanding.

When we open ourselves to the perceptive connection we have to what is Sacred, it is revealed to us in every moment we hold this energy. Before speaking, both Dean and I encountered circumstances of people freeing butterflies trapped indoors and how this tiny act of connection can have such a profound impact (although I believe mine was an incredibly beautiful moth!).

The faces of nature reflect to us that we have many faces of our own; these are represented in the spiritual pathways and in the masks of the Shaman. The spiritual pathways are used in the medicine wheel - the Visionary, the Warrior, the Healer and the Sage.

In order to walk a more wholesome existence, Shamanism offers that we traverse and embody the teachings and qualities of these pathways. It gives us direction and assists in healing and awareness, giving us instruments to embrace a more enriching presence. When we gain more unity in each spiritual space, we are then able to perceive our metaphysical landscapes with more lucidity. For example, when

we are in the role of the educator or the teacher, sometimes the inner critic or the interrogator emerges. Among this land we are learning the terrain and we will swing to the extremes of the pendulum until we come to understand who we are as the Teacher.

When we look at the meaning of being "whole", there are many definitions. One of the qualities of wholeness for me means that we have integrated the different aspects of ourselves. Dean also touches on this. "Find a path that feeds and nourishes you and helps you navigate challenges. The four archetypal paths of the medicine wheel are one illuminating path. In the East we have the Visionary, the teachings to connect to your vision. The North the Warrior, the ability to develop strength and courage and meet the challenges in your life. In the West is the space of the Healer, the Earth Mothers and Grandmothers for healing, and in the South, the Sage, sharing the wisdom you have gained for all beings. The center of the medicine wheel weaves each of these gifts into every person's unique tapestry."

The health of our inner world is nourished by the archetypal paths. These life journeys, lessons and opportunities towards grasping our own wisdom, are shown to us through our everyday life. When connecting to this energy, we can access a greater knowing of who we are, our purpose and our reason for being.

Shamanism reminds us of how we are all connected and how everything is interwoven. It is also the return to love - the dimension of the heart is the doorway between the physical world and the spiritual kingdoms. Our heart speaks to us while we are moving through the voyage of this life. It can speak from within us and through our environment - the greater heart of Mother Nature. When we sit in the space of the heart, it opens us to the world of natural balance. When we are feeling disharmony within our heart space in the form of unhappiness, anger, doubt or other such emotion, our heart is speaking to us of other worlds inside us where deeper gardens are asking to be tended.

Those gardens may be overgrown with weeds and vines that are strangling the life from other plants, or perhaps we perceive some of those inner grounds as the dark forest we hear about in fairytales where unknown creatures lurk. At some stage, weeding, clearing and watering is required.

The paths that we cross give us the opportunity to discover great depth and incredible power. Within each of us sits a considerable truth that we are all connected to, and when we are ready to hear it, it speaks to us with such beauty. When we ask ourselves "What could we do more of to access greater wholeness and harmony in our life?" Perhaps deeper devotion to open more to love and awareness, to hold the self and others with acceptance, appreciation and divinity. Dean shares an apt and elegant quote from Rumi - "Be like the moon - circle what you love."

One of the beautiful qualities I love so much about Spirit is that time is irrelevant. And when the perfect moment presents itself we open another petal of the Lotus flower and, like a child, revel in the magnificence of something so humble yet so profound.

Contact Vicki Dean on (02) 43 561360 or vickidean@aapt.net.au

ANCIENT WISDOM

Laura Naomi is a Contemporary Shaman, which blends the unique modalities of Zen practices, Shamanic and energy healing, space clearing and psychic and emotional counselling. She guides individuals, groups, corporations and businesses and is passionate about creating more awareness around energy and the spiritual world; how it affects us and how to harness this power to create a more harmonious lifestyle. - **Contact Laura at:** Web: www.laura-naomi.com / Email: yourdreams@globaldreamwhisperer.com / Phone: 1300 887 581

The Tree of Life

THE TREE OF LIFE IS A VERY POWERFUL SYMBOL THROUGHOUT MANY CULTURES. IN NORSE MYTHOLOGY IT IS REFERRED TO AS THE YGGDRASIL TREE AND IS BELIEVED TO BE THE CENTRE OF EVERYTHING IN EVERY DIMENSION. IN CELTIC MYTHOLOGY, THE ASH OR 'WORLD TREE' IS A TREE OF ENCHANTMENT AND MAGIC. FOR THIS REASON, MANY WANDS, STAVES AND BESOMS WERE AND ARE STILL MADE FROM THIS TREE. IT IS A MIGHTY TREE, TYPICALLY GROWING UP TO 45 METRES TALL (150 FEET).

The tree's roots are heavily planted into the earth, whilst its branches reach towards the heavens. The Central column spans through the realms and is viewed as the backbone of the universe. The World Tree encompasses the Lower World (Annwn), the Middle World or this world (Abred) and the Upperworld World (Gwynvid). It is said to bridge consciousness from these realms to the physical plane. When a Shaman Journeys, he/she also travels between worlds using the tree of life.

The Tree of Life symbolises a great deal. It teaches us we are made of the earth and of the stars. It also shows how the inner and outer worlds are linked, by taking the sustenance and water from 'within' the earth through its roots, to release oxygen through the leaves into the 'outer' world. It also teaches us about the cycle of life and death. The leaves fall dead to the ground, to then become nourishment for the tree, which creates new growth. It teaches that with death or the end of a cycle, new growth and beginnings ensue, you just need to let go and trust in the process. The tree also shows like a mirror, that is the branches look similar to the roots and if you were to turn the image upside, it would still look like a tree. The tree gives rise to the following 'As Above, so Below, as Within, so Without'.

I have personally worked with each tree of the Celtic Calendar, where each Lunar month is represented by a particular tree. The Ash tree is celebrated on the 5th Lunation, which is February 21 - March 20, keeping in mind that these are dates from where they originated in the Northern Hemisphere. Although I am in the Southern Hemisphere, I found that each tree each month still rang true for me.

Healing with Ash can be very powerful. Call on the energy of Ash when you need to find your centre. Draw on this energy also if you need strength or if you feel alone or isolated. Ash will help you when you are in need of guidance to bring light to a situation.

If you are in need of grounding, the Tree of Life exercise is a very powerful meditation. We often overlook how vitally important it is to ground, especially those that work in spiritual fields. Symptoms we overlook when you need grounding are: clumsiness, un-focused, picking up on others negative emotions, feeling out of sorts, indecisiveness etc. I do the Tree of Life Meditation every morning. You can do it anywhere and it doesn't take long. I even do it on the train into work!

TREE OF LIFE MEDITATION

- Stand with your feet shoulder width apart and knees slightly bent so they are not locked.
- If you are standing, rock back and forth on your feet a little to find a good position so that your balance becomes distributed evenly over your feet. You can also do this lying down or sitting up in a seat.
- Close your eyes and take a few deep breaths to relax and focus. Picture roots growing out of your feet and into the earth.
- Then picture a big white ball of energy in the centre of the earth. Picture light from this ball moving up through the layers of the earth and up through the roots of your feet. Draw the light up through your body to your heart.
- See the light go down to your fingertips and back to your heart. See the light go up through your head and reach up to touch the sun. (If I do this at night I picture it touching the moon)
- Feel the sun on your face as you draw down its white light through your head and trace the way the earth light came through you. Down through your head, to your heart, to your fingertips and back to your heart, down through your body, out through your feet, through the roots and connect with the ball of white light in the centre of the earth.
- Now that you have connected like the tree of life, it is important to shield yourself. This helps deflect any negative energies.
- You can picture a big white bubble in front of you that you step into, or maybe a shield pops up all around you. I picture impenetrable light shields around me (three in fact, I'm not sure why I chose three, just go with whatever feels right for you). Fill your shield full of white light and know you are protected.

If you are interested in the Celtic Tree Calendar, I highly recommend the book 'The Healing Power of Trees' by Sharlyn Hidalgo. It is a practical book where Sharlyn takes you through meditations to connect with each tree and discover their teachings. There is a beautiful meditation in there to connect with the Ash 'your centre'. You will discover a lot about yourself in this process and it's only 1-2 trees per lunar month. I kept a journal of each tree. My meditation with the Ash tree was beautiful. I realised that I am a lot stronger than I thought. I discovered that regardless of what has happened to me over the years, I still remain strong and on purpose. I connected with my heart's truth and understood that spirituality and nature give me the most joy and happiness.

GODDESS INSPIRATION

ANCIENT WISDOM

Harmonia - GREEK GODDESS OF HARMONY AND CONCORD

Harmonia was the daughter of Aphrodite and Ares' adulterous affair. Harmonia is said to have brought harmony to marital matters and war and was also mentioned as a deity that presided over the cosmic harmony. However Harmonia was gifted on her wedding day with a cursed necklace that was to doom her descendants with endless tragedy. She is often depicted in relief work receiving this necklace that is famously referred to as the Necklace of Harmonia, which brought hardship to all who possessed it, although it was said to never have an effect on her.

Draw the energy of Harmonia to you when you need to find balance in your life. Her message is to first look within yourself. What you put forth from within will create your external environment. Find your peace and balance by being still and listening to your own soul. Meditate for Harmonia to show you the way, she will be your guide, but ultimately it is up to you to do the work. Once you find your centre and balance within yourself, you cannot be shaken. No matter what life or others throw at you, it will have no effect. Stand strong in your own power.

Nicola is an Artist, Herbalist and Pagan. As she is learning to walk the Shamans Path she is ever learning and evolving, acquiring knowledge from many faiths and origins. She has a special affinity with Celtic lore and everything Faery. Her connection to Nature and Spirit is what drives her to grow and motivates her to teach.

Please contact Nicola at: www.nicolamcintosh.com / nicola@nicolamcintosh.com

Artwork Credit: Nicola McIntosh

THE POWER OF A NAME

Reilly McCarron reveals how relating stories as medicine, fairy tales can be used to reflect the struggles we face in life, bringing understanding, healing and closure…

Carl Jung, the founder of Analytical Psychology, believed that a person could become their true self through a process of 'individuation'. This involves illuminating the unconscious parts of ourselves in an effort to gain wholeness through integration. Or, to put it another way, lighting lanterns in the deep dark psyche to shed the soft glow of self knowledge. Clear insights into the shadowy inner world allow us to reclaim lost, forgotten and rejected fragments of who we really are, as we slowly put the pieces together and 're-member' our true selves.

Jung pioneered his influential style of psychology by tracing the symbols and motifs found in dreams, art, myth and fairy tales. Since the early days of psychoanalysis fairy tales have been used to map the unknown psyche, and continue to illuminate the strange and enchanted inner realms to this day. However, rather than each fairy tale revealing a standard set of insights, the meaning drawn from a tale can be different for each person, even changing for the same person at different times of their life. There is no single correct way to interpret the rich symbolism of a fairy tale.

In her book Tell It by Heart: Women and the Healing Power of Story, Erica Helm Meade uses stories as medicine. The book presents a series of fascinating case studies, including one which explores the story of 'Rumpelstiltskin'. This deceptively simple tale resonates with Faye; a woman who is suffering from Chronic Fatigue Syndrome. Faye is a driven academic, an overachiever, who suddenly finds herself unable to fulfill simple tasks after a lifetime of pushing herself to succeed.

In the fairy tale a poor miller boasts that his daughter can spin straw into gold. Hearing this, the king decides to test the girl - if she succeeds she will become his queen, but if she fails she will be put to death. During counselling Faye reveals that her own father held similarly unrealistic expectations of her, leading to a manic ambition which eventually left her burnt out. Over time Faye recognises the entire cast of fairy tale characters within herself, as Helm Meade guides her to a sense of inner peace.

While Faye's insights are invaluable to her, there is another meaning to be drawn from the tale. When it comes time for the girl to spin gold, the hopeless task brings her to tears. Then in walks a little imp who offers to help her in exchange for whatever she has to offer - at first this is jewelry, but it soon escalates to her first born child. In desperation the girl agrees, but when she becomes queen and her child is born she begs the tiny man for mercy. He agrees to allow her three days to guess his name, and if she succeeds the ghastly deal will be broken.

The human mind is amazingly clever and resourceful, and when faced with trauma it constructs coping (or defense) mechanisms to see us through until we reach safe ground once more. Faced with a death sentence, the girl in the story is aided by a magical helper who will do the impossible work for her. Psychologically speaking this may mean we dissociate, embrace denial or delusion, act out of character, fall prey to substance abuse or find another form of temporary collapse while some hidden part of ourselves steps up to face the challenge. For a while the price we pay is relatively small, but not for long. Soon enough the magical helper turns into a greedy goblin. Only if we name it in time will we be spared its outrageous demands. Only if we recognise it for what it is, and reclaim our power once we are on safe ground will we find our happily ever after.

All too often temporary coping mechanisms become ingrained and normalised. We react as though in danger, and may even seek danger, failing to recognise when we have reached safety and become strong. The thing that got us through a difficult time now demands possession of our most precious creations. Yet gaining enough insight to discern our own magical helpers and voracious villains allows us to re-integrate them into our whole selves.

The insights you draw from fairy tales, or art or dreams, are the most significant for you at the time. So allow yourself to light a few lanterns in the dark woods and to ponder over what you find there.

Reilly McCarron is the creator and enchantress of 'faerie bard', and President of the Australian Fairy Tale Society. She is a singer/songwriter, a Bard with the Order of Bards, Ovates and Druids (OBOD), an accredited member of the Australian Storytelling Guild (NSW) and has a Graduate Diploma in Australian Folklore with a particular interest in fairy tales. Contact Reilly at: Email: austfairytales@gmail.com Web: www.facebook.com/austfairytales

What is Buddhism

By Nicole Humber – Jigme Radnamaya

Buddha means Awaken One, "Enlightenment".

Buddhism is the way or path to Enlightenment, Awakening. When the great Universal teacher Shakyamuni Buddha first spoke about Dharma (Law of Nature) in the noble land of India, he taught the four noble truths - the truth of suffering, the cause of suffering, the path leading to the cessation of suffering, and the cessation of suffering.

These profound teachings are timeless. If one truly sits and observes life, one might first see beauty and wonder but looking closely, will recognise suffering is all around. Birth, sickness, old age and death, this is suffering. Attachment, anger, desire and ignorance all lead and cause suffering. These stem from our mind and create negative speech and action.

Being aware of the way we think, how we speak and use our actions can transform our lives and the lives around us in a very positive way. Just simplifying our lives in this busy chaotic world can bring great clarity. Really being grateful for what we have right now in our lives, breeds contentment.

Do we need to give animals untimely deaths to satisfy our hunger? We are able to live very healthily on fruit and vegetables alone, so why do we choose to eat so much animal flesh? Greed is one aspect of ignorance.

To be truly happy, one is best living in equanimity, finding a balance where harmony and wholeness reside. Accumulating wisdom and insight opens ones heart to compassionate action. We humans have a great deal of potential to develop universal compassion and kindness.

Understanding that every one of us including all other living beings are a member of cyclic existence. In other words, we are all in the same boat, same situation. Live to love and watch the magic of the Buddha, Dharma bestow blessings.

May all beings benefit.

Inspired by my precious teacher The 12th Gyalwang Drukpa, the head teacher of the Drukpa Kargyu lineage of Tibetan Buddhism. Nicole Humber can be contacted at email: radnamaya@live.com

Cosmic Codes
with Amanda Coppa

Moon Magic for the months ahead.

April 2014

An energetically powerful month with both a full moon lunar eclipse in Libra on the 15th followed by a new moon solar eclipse in Taurus on the 29th. The full moon places an intense focus on personal transformation, healing and self-acceptance. Now is the time to let go of the past and become aware of how we give and receive love. Eclipses usher in periods of change and potent energy shifts that can have long lasting effects. Do your best not to get too far ahead of yourself and trust in perfect timing. Take a step back and observe yourself and your personal relationships with more clarity.

The new moon in Taurus sets the emotional landscape for the next four weeks, and emphasises the need for self-healing, strengthening self-love and readying ourselves for an inflow of new energy. The solar eclipse will bring about some sort of 'personal crisis' that ultimately leads to positive change. Love and relationships are highlighted and we are encouraged to lay strong foundations for more empowered connections and partnerships. Feeling our way, trusting the flow and taking inspired action is key to working with this energy.

May 2014

A highly spiritual and insightful month with the full moon in Scorpio on the 15th followed by a new moon in Gemini on the 29th. This full moon reminds us to keep it simple, relax and be guided by our inner wisdom. At times it can be hard to see the wood for the trees, and we are being reminded to release our hold and trust that everything is coming together as it should. Hidden fears or self-sabotaging tendencies may surface now. Gently let them go and know that you have everything you need now to guide you to the next stage in your life.

CONT'D PAGE 25

Amanda Coppa is a heart-centred crystal healer who incorporates astrology, numerology, Reiki and oracle cards into her work. She is passionate about self-healing, empowerment and helping you understand the REAL you. Connect with Amanda at http://www.facebook.com/cosmiccodes.

Spirit Guide Wisdom

A place of serenity and abundant growth. Spirit is guiding you forth with the highest potential for an abundant increase in your spiritual growth and understanding. Much of this growth will be achieved through your emotions. Hence the water feature represented here. As the water feeds the growth abundantly by the banks of the garden, so too does your emotion feed your personal growth. Nature always provides what is needed for this growth to take place. So, trust that the Universe and your Spirit Guide will provide what is needed for you to achieve this growth.

You will find that you will be given all that is required to enable you to achieve the full potential of growth. This will include the right experiences and people. While, at times it may not be a peaceful garden to be in, know that behind the beauty of God's Garden the universe is working very hard to achieve the growth you see

Artwork is by Nicolle Poll of Artwork by Nicolle and part of the Spirit Guide Wisdom Oracle card set with author Kerrie Wearing. To be published in 2015

Centered in Oneness

Centering yourself in Oneness and Connection has never been more simplified with this offering by Kerrie Wearing.
© Anthony Hathaway | Dreamstime Stock Photos

The art of knowing oneself in the likeness of God is often thought to be more difficult than we realize. Becoming centered, feeling your way to inspiration, finding that place within you that speaks of peace, harmony and your connection to the Divine is still somewhat illusive for many of us, moment to moment and day to day.

So we traipse off to this workshop and that retreat, attend meditation groups, all the while searching for something that is already there within us.

We just need to know it for ourselves in a way that is intimate, easy, and so relevant that we never forget that it is there.

For me there is only one way to achieve this kind of connection and knowing, and that is through the experience of it. As with all things in life we never forget how we feel when we are having a worthwhile experience. Whether it's the good, bad or the ugly, we always remember.

Well, I can assure you that a daily experience of knowing you are centered in Oneness with this great Universe is a joyful experience. One where you see life flow with ease and grace, one where you feel a sense of purpose to life and one where maintaining this connection is at the forefront of your heart, soul and mind once you experience it.

The Key is to derive a simple, passive expression of it in your life that speaks to you in a way that melds easily with your life. Other peoples' expressions may not work for you and that is OK. Give yourself permission to find your own truth, even if that truth is 'I'm not ready yet'. Only truth and honesty with yourself will set you free here. Any self-delusion will have you forever stuck in the confines of ego and all that that entails - misery.

I offer you from my life experience a simple exercise that only needs to be done once, yet can be carried with you for all time as a reminder when your emotions and life get a little tough.

Take your journal, or even grab a copy of my Wisdom of the Soul Creative Intentions Journal which houses a space for this very exercise.

Step 1: Align yourself with the Divine in whatever way works for you - prayer, meditation, yoga, music, a walk on the beach. It really does not matter how you achieve this as long as you feel uplifted, centered and Joyful, and that your Spirit, which is that part of you which is inherently connected to the Divine, is present, while your ego is at rest for now. Even if this is proving difficult, fear not, as the exercise itself will help to align you in the moment.

Step 2: Now with your journal, answer this very simple question by writing down the immediate response. Do not think, just write as the thoughts, feelings and pictures flow.

IN ONENESS I AM…………

Centered in Oneness

A cleansing ritual to call your Spirit & Soul back to wholeness
by Kerrie Wearing

PERSONAL GROWTH

This visualization is designed to gather your soul by calling back your Spirit and all the pieces of your Soul, which are energetically entwined with people, places and circumstances that do not serve you, which could be causing physical and emotional disturbances within your soul, or at the very least detracting from your sense of peace.

- Imagine yourself in a field on a beautiful summer's day. In this field you feel the warmth of the sun's rays and are becoming mindful of all that nature is offering, around you. You notice the field of wildflowers and any animals that may also be residents of your field.
- As you look around, to the left you notice a small, gentle waterfall with a very inviting pool of water. So inviting in fact, you can't wait to immerse yourself and feel the water all over you.
- So you hurry along and before you know it, you are standing right in the depths of this glorious waterfall, showering yourself with all that it has to offer.
- Immediately you begin to feel like your true self as the water washes away all your worries, cares and anything troubling your mind. With this you really start to relax and you notice your breathing start to slow.
- Standing beneath this waterfall, you feel a growing presence of strength and centeredness while your connection to the Divine is becoming all encompassing. In this moment your sense of power is growing. Yet there is more.
- In this moment you slowly start to become aware that there are parts of your energy entwined throughout your universe that may not be beneficial, serving you well or even quite distinctly detracting from the wholeness of your Spirit & Soul.
- As the knowingness of each instance arrives into your awareness, speak mindfully to your Soul requesting its return home with these words:

"Divine Spirit of me, I love you and care for you so deeply, that I no longer wish for you to engage in energies, be it people, places or circumstances that do not lift us up and hold our being in love and joy.
Please come back to me in Wholeness and Harmony."

- Do this for each instance that arises. As you feel this come to its completion, please take some more time to continue cleansing beneath your waterfall and embrace all that you are with love.
- When you feel the time is right, allow the imagery to dissipate and return your awareness to the room you are in and your body, and in your own time, opening your eyes.

Time now to journal, have a cuppa and enJOY the Wisdom of your Soul.

Converse with your Spirit in this way as you would any other being. Feel the heart of who you are. What is your Divine Purpose in being here? You know all of this, you only need ask in simple, yet specific terms.

Step 3: Having now seen yourself in the likeness of God, begin a new way of being by seeing this expressed throughout your life.

For one week, in your journal at the end of every day, write down where you have seen how your sense of Oneness and connection to the Divine is woven throughout your life. Where you have experienced moments of Joy, Love and inSpiration. Where what is important to you has been expressed throughout your day.

And lastly, if your aim is to enhance your life by wanting to see more of these moments in your life, then keep journaling at the end of every day until you no longer feel the need. This act will keep your focus, attention and therefore creative energy on the positive and Spirit-filled attributes of your life, thereby increasing and expanding its hold on your life. And there you have the Soul's desire being fulfilled.

I invite you to visit our inSpirit Magazine Facebook page and tell us how you get along. I and the team would love to hear how your sense of being Centered in Oneness is working for you.

Kerrie Wearing is an internationally recognised Soul Coach and Medium, specialising in coaching and mentoring people to connect with their unique Soul Purpose. She is the author of A New Kind of Normal; Unlock the Medium Within, managing editor of inSpirit Magazine and director of inSpirit Publishing. Website: www.kerriewearing.com

Shell Healing for Health, Happiness and Harmony

Our Wisdom Keeper of Oceanic Mysteries, Gem~mer, unveils the hidden power of working with Shell Magic, the Bones of the Seas…..

As the bones of the Sea wash unto me, I am grateful for the way that they touch my heart, grateful for the way that they touch my soul and oh so grateful for the balance they bring to me. Living in harmony with the gifts that Nature offers, with the gifts that are offered from the belly of the sea, is a union that offers as much wonderment as it does peace and harmony, and the stories that seashells tell - amazing!

Stories of journeys and other-worlds, of life and love, of experience and gratitude. Tales of sadness and despair and stories of ancient ways of healing, of balancing and creating harmony, of creating happiness in one's body and soul.

As these stories unfold between my ears and within my heart, I often ponder why it is that I hear them so well; the response that I receive from the spirit of the Sea is always the same; to share it with the world. So share it I will!

The spiritual journey of harnessing shell energy leads to creating balance in one's life. Finding peace, living harmoniously and feeling complete and whole, is something that most of us strive for. An understanding, recognition of the balancing act needed to achieve this. To feel in complete harmony with ourselves and our surroundings, is something that our friends from the sea can guide us to.

Shells of the sea hold an amazing amount of energy, an energy signature unique unto themselves. Imprinted with their own unique birthright energy, infused with the energetic imprint of the sea creature that once called it home, imbued with the life journey of the mollusc and the journey of reaching us on the shoreline all factor in to the energetic imprint of sea bones, creating a unique energetic quality.

There is too, a general energy pertaining to each seashell family, one that we can harness and explore confidently, one that we can utilise for healing, for bringing peace, for creating balance and harmony within our daily lives. A simple meditation or visualisation can be a powerful ally in creating harmony within your soul and what better place to begin then in your sacred heart space. So let's open up and allow the Heart Cockle to weave its magic on your soul.

Sacred Heart Cockle Visualisation:

Gather your Heart Cockle shell (in your hand or your mind's eye) and find a nice, quiet space where you won't be disturbed. Close your eyes and breathe in deeply. Exhale. Breathe in deeply and release until you are feeling relaxed and centred.

In your mind's eye or in the physical realm, hold your Heart Cockle shell cupped in your hands. Allow your sacred heart space to open in beautiful waves of watery pinks. Open your heart space wider and wider. Lift your Heart Cockle shell and hold it to your heart. Allow it to enter your heart space, breathe the Heart Cockle deep into your heart. See the Heart Cockle shell filling your heart with love, infusing its gentle yet powerful energy. Allow the Heart Cockle to spread into your heart space, see it reaching into the deep recesses of your beautiful heart knowing that she is weaving her magick, weaving her harmonious magick within you. Take the time to allow yourself, your sacred heart space, to connect with the healing energy of the Heart Cockle shell.

When you feel ready, begin to visualise her release, her pulling back into herself, her moving outside of your heart space and back into your hands.

Breathe in deeply. Exhale. Breathe in deeply. Release. Breathe in deeply, exhale and slowly open your eyes.

An audio of this visualisation is available to download for FREE at http://bit.ly/1aIuWxd

Side note: On my journey, I never take 'living' shells and I would always advise against doing so out of respect and love for all creatures, great and small. I would like to urge you to only gather 'used' shells from our beaches.

For those who wish to buy shells, my advice is to source ethical suppliers. Ask the hard questions such as how the shells are sourced and connect with one that suits your personal ethics best.

If you like searching through Op Shops, salvaging shells can be done knowing that you are honouring the sea creature once held within.

~May the Wisdom and Magick of Ocean and Sea's Inspire Us All~

Gem~mer is an Ocean Enchantress, Intuitive Creatress and Teacher of Ocean Magicks. Gem's creative works include crafting ocean talismans and tools for spiritual connections and teaching ocean magicks through magazine articles, workshops and online courses. Gem~mer has also begun the magickal journey of creating oracle and insight decks, books and birthing illuminating retreats as a way of sharing and teaching the magick and wisdom of ocean and sea's. 'May the Wisdom and Magick of Ocean and Sea's Inspire Us All'. www.cryshellmagic.com.au

Everyday Enchantment with the Elements

Living altars formed by Nature, sacred circles drawn, blessed elements called upon, for pure magic to be borne - Natasha Heard steps us deeply and simply into this most wondrous realm…

With my magical amethyst staff in one hand and a basket of sacred spell casting treasures in the other, I gently step barefooted through the long grass, ducking under branches and bending to not disturb the spider's webs woven between the shrubs and trees.

With each step the energy grows finer but yet - stronger. My curiosity is ignited as I feel my aura becoming brighter, lighter and I am totally grounded. I surrender to Spirit; I know I am getting closer and closer. I trust and I am guided to a place in between our reality and the realms of magic.

In the enchanted bush land behind my home I have found a natural altar and blessing bowl that is a living, breathing Gum Tree! I know in my bones I have been guided to perform my magical spell right here and so I walk clockwise around this living altar and use my staff to draw a sacred circle, a place between this world and the realms of magic. I stand next to my tree friend who connects me down deep to Mother Earth and stretches up towards Father Sky. In my mind words swirl around and around, almost a whisper unspoken… earth… air… fire… water… I form the words and then I speak, I call them into my circle… EARTH! AIR! FIRE! WATER! COME NEAR TO AID GAIA'S DAUGHTER… I feel their energy rush to me and around me kissing my skin and then settling into their space within my circle. I feel they have come from so far away and yet they were always with me, always.

I cast my spell; I send it out into the Universe, knowing my words have been heard. I make offerings to the Goddess Gaia and thank her for all I have, all I am and all that is coming into my life. I thank the elements one by one for joining me and I open my circle by retracing the invisible circling line backwards with my staff just like an eraser taking pencil off paper, it has disappeared and I feel the elements rush away with my wishes.

I step back towards my home and back into the mundane world. Each step toward my home, it is like forgetting a fantastical dream. I remember the groceries I need to collect from the shops, my appointments for that afternoon and what I will be doing the following day, but in my heart and my soul the magic remains. I know my spell will magically manifest and I smile.

This kind of spell casting does not happen every day in my life, but when I am in need of divine help or have some BIG wishes to cast out, I will go to that special tree and I call on the elements and Goddess Gaia to aid me. My usual days are full of "normal" tasks such as housework and getting school lunches ready BUT I see every part of my life as magical and as a natural witch every word spoken and every action is an ongoing mini spell!

I magically manifest my future every minute of the day and so can YOU! Keeping in touch with all of the elements can help in everyday manifestation. Breathing deeply, burning incense and wearing feathers in your hair connect you to the element Air.

Putting clothes on the line is the perfect opportunity to ground and feel our Mother Earth under your feet, eating root vegetables and having crystals the home and in jewellery connects to the element Earth.

Walking on the beach, swimming in the river or even simply washing up is connecting to Water and burning candles, cooking food and being passionate about life connects to Fire!

By keeping these magical elements balanced every day we become in tune with spirit and our thoughts and actions create our nearest and furthest future. Keep your thoughts positive, fantasise and daydream, see yourself living the life you have always wished for and watch as your life magically manifests in all its glory.

Natasha Heard is a creatress of all things magical! A natural witch ~ her magical life and connection to the Earth flow into all her creations. Specialising in Wands, Sceptres and Staves; and creating with her horticulturalist husband Michael, Blessed Rune sets and Tree of Life Bind Rune Talismans. Her innate connection with all aspects of the natural world and passion for magic is what makes her a true creatress of powerful, magical tools. Natasha can be contacted at: www.blessedbranches.com Email: blessedbranches@gmail.com or flowerlove@live.com.au / Facebook: Blessed Branches…magical tools by Natasha Heard. Artwork Credit - Nicolle Poll www.facebook.com/ArtworkByNicolle

Living with Spirit

By Kerrie Wearing

An extract from A New Kind of Normal: Unlock the Medium Within by Kerrie Wearing (published by inSpirit Publishing)

When we first begin to raise our spiritual awareness and understand there is more to this life than we first perceived, we begin to notice universal signs and an increased amount of seemingly co-incidental occurrences. Almost as if the universe is whispering to you.

In doing so, we slowly begin to think of ourselves as spiritual beings. In fact, there is a common expression used in the spiritual community "We are spiritual beings having a physical experience." While I believe this to be true, I also think the use of this expression is quite often bandied about with little thought for what the words truly mean or what living such a concept would be like.

If we are a spirit first and a human second, what do you think life would look like for you or for someone who truly lives from that perspective?

In my experience they are someone who easily understands that the way forward is always through love. While they may still encounter difficulties in life, their ability to approach these challenges seeking insight and understanding is first and foremost their priority, as not only do they know this is where all solutions lie, but they also inherently know that their souls only purpose is one of learning, evolution and enlightenment.

They would see through the illusion to the truth and the heart of matters, while easily seeing the essence of people. Seeing the light in all, even those clouded in darkness and not let judgement stand in their way.

To visit Kerrie: www.kerriewearing.com / Facebook: www.facebook.com/authorkerriewearing
A New Kind of Normal is available on Amazon, all the ebook stores and via Kerrie's website.

If we are a Spirit first and a human second what do you think life would look like for you or for someone who truly lives from that perspective? inSpired by her own journey of living with Spirit, Kerrie shares with you her personal inSights on how living with Spirit can transform your life.

They heed the call of their own heart knowing that to love thyself is a symbol of loving God and this great universe, for in so doing they are loving all of creation. While living this, they are mindful of giving to others but not to the point of self sacrifice as this hinders the ability to love freely.

Turning away from engaging in negativity and supplying any energy to such matters, becomes a natural instinct as they seek to maintain an energy of positivity, joy and upliftment. Knowing their own Spirit rejoices in this as well as being fully aware of the energetic contribution they make to those around them and the Universe as a whole.

Baring in mind the intricacies of this world, each and every one of us can express all of this quite differently, from simple smiles, loving gestures with a mindfulness and awareness as one goes about raising their children and providing for their family. To others who feel a greater call to share this knowledge and understanding with others, so they too can rejoice and walk with peace and understanding.

Life itself will flow more easily with this awareness of living from our Spirit. The universe leads us forward consciously through the flow of synchronicity, God's lighted pathway as I like to call it, which is more commonly recognised as those 'co-incidences' that cross our path. I prefer the term synchronicity as to me it feels that I am valuing this in my life more whereas using the term 'co-incidences'tends to devalue the true essence, giving the event or occurrence almost a flippant view of it. When really, nothing could be further from the truth.

Living from your Spirit will naturally bring about a sense of harmony resulting in a life of balance, spiritual maturity and a flow of regularly occurring synchronistic events designed to move you forward to achieving your true life's purpose. You won't even need to try. There is no hard work about making this happen, apart from living your true Spirit. While this at times may not always be easy for a variety of reasons, such as not living to other people's expectations of you, even if they most likely are family. Or often having the realisation that in this moment you are not truly happy, and that it is only you letting yourself down in some way. Someone living with Spirit knows that in facing life's challenges there is ALWAYS a higher purpose and we need only to look for it.

For a long time now, I have been at peace with my brother's suicide. Once I began opening up spiritually I was always of the understanding that without that experience and his loss, I wouldn't be who I am today. This is something I still feel today and while there was and still is some pain, he really gave me the greatest gift of all. Myself!

(Tears flowing just now... as I thank him yet again.)

Going forward over the next couple of days, I shall be mindful of watching for all the car registration plates which have the letter KEZ on them. This is one of his regular signs to me which symbolises he is around and that everything is ok. He called me "Kezza" and was the only one to do so and is now the only one allowed to.

In your life there will be many ways like this that Spirit will begin the first stages of communicating with you. This is not only to reassure us, but to also remind us that we are spiritual beings ourselves. Over the years I have heard many, many stories regarding signs and synchronicities which involve music, animals, birds, butterflies, feathers and much more. There was even one father a little more keen to get his message across than that.This was a few years ago when I still did face to face readings at home. I was sitting with Angela and was making a connection to her father Ron. The names have been changed to protect their privacy. During this session, there were two magical moments that happened.

I said to Angela that Ron made himself known at home by the presence of physical activity such as lights flickering and doors opening. Well it was only a moment or two later that the door opened to the room we were in. I had never experienced this door opening of its own fruition before, so I understood this to be Ron's way to let his daughter Angela now that it truly was him, as what was to come next was extremely important.

Ron was quite an astute man and was quick to know and recognise my boundaries as a medium, thereby delivering the next message without me realising it. I continued, saying to Angela that her dad was quite proud to see that she was keeping her father's memory alive in her little boy. He showed me a picture of a little boy praying, indicating that he could see his grandson praying to him at night before bed. He went onto to say that as the little boy grows, her dad will forever be in this little boys heart. This was a nice sentiment I thought, but one which had so much more meaning to Angela. At the end of the session, Angela shared with me that her son needed a heart transplant and with Ron saying he would grow in her son's heart, she understood this to be her dad's way of telling her the new heart was coming, and he was right. I heard a few months later that the little boy did indeed receive his new heart and all was going well.

PSYCHIC AWARENESS

Kerrie Wearing is an internationally recognised Soul Coach and Medium, specialising in coaching and mentoring people to connect with their unique Soul Purpose. She is the author of A New Kind of Normal; Unlock the Medium Within, managing editor of inSpirit Magazine and director of inSpirit Publishing. She is currently working on her second book Wisdom of the Soul.

For the love of Angels
By Suzanne Hartas

THE ANGELS OF HARMONY
SAY THAT HARMONY IS A BALANCE BETWEEN THE SPIRITUAL, EMOTIONAL AND PHYSICAL PLANES.

The Angels say "My Dearly Beloved, it is possible to live your Spirit on Earth; you need not pass from this world to the next to know the love, peace, freedom and union with your spirit. For you see Dear One's, your spirit cannot leave you nor you leave it. With the recognition of this truth, the wholeness and perfection of you is undeniable. Your spirit is a creation from the one pure light of all perfection, 'The Divine Light.' When accepting and acknowledging this truth to one self, it will take much courage to admit that the protective shield of your imagined imperfections has never really existed.

It is you and only you who are responsible for the theatre of your life. Know that it is you who holds the power as creator, writer and director of the script you call your life. For each and every scene of your existence has been a manifestation of your thoughts, so we ask Dear One's; be mindful of the thoughts you project and the words that you speak, for they are indeed the seeds of creation.

When this truth has been realized the key to your freedom will turn, as you escape from the illusion of boundaries and limitations, which have hindered you from truly living the expression of your authentic self. As in Heaven you will again return to experiencing a peaceful, joyous and harmonious existence, for you will truly be living your Heaven on Earth. When you recognize that you are Spirit within Life, peace will truly be yours Dear One's.

Much love and many blessings."

Susanne Hartas is a Psychic Medium and Angel Intuitive.

Please contact Suzanne at:
www.inspiritmagazine.com
mail@inspiritmagazine.com

CERTIFICATE OF SHAMANISM & TRANSFORMATIONAL MASK
open and deepen your relationship to the sacred, attuning your being to the song of land and spirit

Shamanism is founded in deep spirituality and a respect for all life. It is practised in some form in all indigenous earth-based cultures. We are all descendents of a shamanic culture; we carry within us shamanic potential. This Certificate course introduces shamanic practice:
* The Medicine Wheel
* Shamanic Journeying
* Divination
* Chakra Healing
* Ritual
* Dream Wisdom
* Sacred Art
* Trance Dance
* Mask and Movement

Limited participants to ensure individual attention throughout the course.

Part A of the IICT Accredited Diploma course so graduates can obtain Professional Indemnity & Public Liability

For Bookings or enquires contact:

Vicki Dean on 02 4356 1360 / email: vickidean@aapt.net.au or

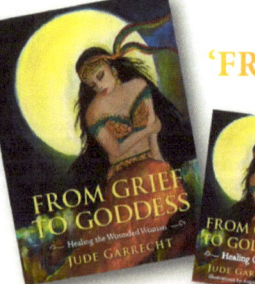

Jude Garrecht, author of **'FROM GRIEF TO GODDESS'** book and Healing Cards now offers workshops and talks on living the life of your dreams throughout Australia and New Zealand.

Visit www.fromgrieftogoddess.com for details or to order your copy of **'FROM GRIEF TO GODDESS'** today!

Come and visit Jude at the CONSCIOUS LIVING EXPO
Melbourne April 25-27 / Sydney May 23 - 25

Gift of being a Sensitive

Kye Crow shares a powerful life lesson and why it is so important for those that are Earthworkers, Lightworkers, Sensitives and Empaths to recognise and be in your own power...

It's almost twenty years ago that my partner Gill and I were dropping off some rubbish at our local tip when my attention was drawn to a cassette tape lying in the dirt. It had no label so I had no idea what it was about, but something deep inside me knew it was important. I put it in the car stereo immediately.

This unexpected gift was about the life of Elizabeth Kubler-Ross, an amazing woman who worked with sick and dying children. Through these children's artwork she could interpret that on some level they knew they were about to die and what it was they needed to resolve before they did. For one little boy, it was simply a desire to ride his bike without trainer wheels. Elizabeth was able to be a bridge between these children and their grieving parents who were often and very understandably in denial.

Listening to the voice of this extraordinary woman and hearing about the children she worked with bought up so much emotion for Gill and I we actually had to pull over and park for a while. I was deeply moved by what she said but there was one thing that I have never ever forgotten. It has been a key that has transformed the way I experience my reality and it came when Elizabeth addressed the question of how she managed to help these children and NOT emotionally break down.

What I understood was that she was able to be present with these children because she had healed her own pain and that when we cry, for whatever reason, the tears we shed are always our own.

Hearing this was like a light going on for me and from that day on I saw my gift of sensitivity in a totally different way. Up until then I had often felt burdened by my ability to feel life and all its woes, so acutely.

I know that living on planet earth with its harsh vibration and all its pain can be a challenge for empaths and sensitives like me, but I have come to realise that being a sensitive is a gift and it was given to us to be used in these times of planetary transformation.

We are the bridges between the unseen realms, the animals, the tree and stone beings, the crystals and Fae and Mother Earth herself. When a tree is felled we can channel the energy of that tree back into the earth to aid the bushes and plants that surround it and help soothe the violence that the tree felt when being cut, but whether we are an earth healer and animal communicator, a guardian of deaths threshold, a wise woman, a witch, or a voice for the elementals, the gifts that we each have are many and varied and cannot be practiced in a clear and conscious way if we are overwhelmed with sorrow or engulfed in the suffering we see on the planet.

Whatever comes up and overwhelms me is MINE and the clearer I get the more I am able to be present in LOVE and compassion to the pain and suffering of others, especially the injured and abused animals that find their way to our sanctuary.

I no longer blame my pain or affliction on the planetary alignment or the latest solar flare. Of course these events impact us but they only bring up what's there within us. Only when we own these aspects of ourselves and take responsibility for them, can we heal.

Our Mother Earth needs her earth workers, her sensitives and empaths to be in their power. Even if someone else provokes us, how we choose to respond is up to us, but nothing can wobble us from our centre when we are in a space of love/light.

When I get out of balance now, I know it is because somewhere, I have not honoured me. I have not rested when I was tired, or eaten that green salad when my body craved it, or drunk enough pure water to flush my body out.

When there are lots of erratic planetary influences I spend as much time in nature as I can earthing myself, walking barefoot or sitting beside a tree.

I treasure my sensitivity now as the Sacred gift it is and the more I am able to take responsibility for my own responses and reactions, the more energy I have to give, to those I am here to help, the animals.

Kye Crow is the Creatress of Wunjo Crow, a range of Goddess clothing that's sprinkled with love and sewn with magic. Kye and her partner Gill live with over a 100 rescued animals and teach Sacred Journeys into the Animal Realms, the power of Love and how to live on planet earth as a sensitive.
Contact Kye at: Web: www.camelcampsanctuary.com / Facebook: www.facebook.com/Wunjocrow
Photo Credit: Argnesh Rose Visionary Digital Artist specialising in fantasy and totem portraiture – www.givethemwings.com.au

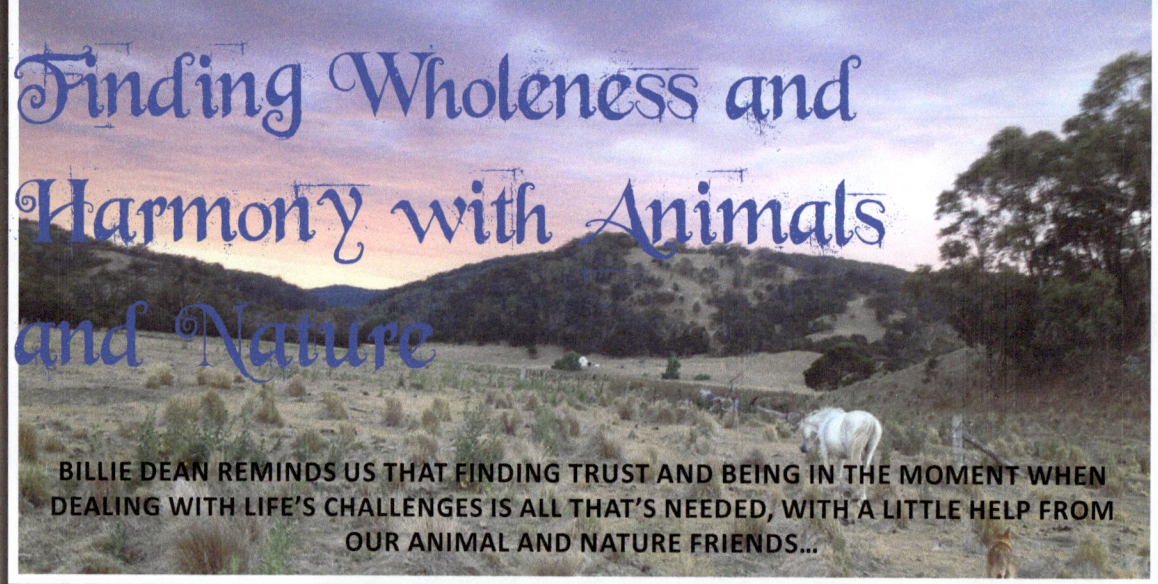

Finding Wholeness and Harmony with Animals and Nature

BILLIE DEAN REMINDS US THAT FINDING TRUST AND BEING IN THE MOMENT WHEN DEALING WITH LIFE'S CHALLENGES IS ALL THAT'S NEEDED, WITH A LITTLE HELP FROM OUR ANIMAL AND NATURE FRIENDS...

SHAMANISM

IT'S DROUGHT TIME AND THE LANDSCAPE IS BLEAK IN ITS DUSTY BROWN. THE LACK OF RAIN HAS AN IMPACT. THE PILE OF WASHING GROWS LARGER. SO DOES THE WASHING UP. WE SHOWER LESS. ANYTHING WE CAN DO TO LIVE MORE LIGHTLY WHILE WAITING FOR THE RAIN.

The outside animals start calling "feed me", cows looking hopefully at you, and sheep chase the car when you drive through their paddock. "You do have hay in there. Don't you?" You don't have to be an animal telepath to work out that it is time to start hand-feeding again.

My husband and I are standing by our old mustard yellow troopy which we use to cart the hay in, discussing hand-feeding options. There isn't much choice – 300 animals once a day, 100 animals twice a day – until the others tell us they need more, I'm haunted by thoughts sent to me by kangaroos. "This is our country" they say. I used to leave them the mountains in the drought so they could have something, even if it meant 100 less acres for our rescues who can eat hay. I'm feeling as bleak as the landscape. The animals do love their hay, but they do so much better on their natural diet. And what about the wild life? My thoughts take a slow dive.

But then something tells me to look up. Two eagles soaring just overhead, right above us. "Have faith" they say. I shake my head and smile a real smile. Stop worrying. We both laugh. The lesson I really learnt last year was all about staying in the moment and not letting fear thoughts send you scuttling into a future that might never be. An old spiritual maxim for sure. But now I could really see how it only led to darkness. I put the brakes on those thoughts now.

Just for today there is a happily flowing creek. Just for today there is enough hay for everyone. Just for today there are eagles and magic. Be in the moment. And if the next moment isn't as good as you had hoped, roll up your acceptance sleeves. It is what it is. Take appropriate action for every moment. And focus on the kind of world you do want. I visualised green.

Trusting in the Divine has never been my strong point. It's a lesson my animals have been trying to get me to get for decades. So when brumby Taliesan told me he was finished healing the major wound on his leg, and I heard but didn't let him go, he jumped the fence and let himself out of intensive care.

I knew he was okay, but I went looking for him anyway and the brumby herd took me to a beautiful oasis. There were purple flowers and green grass and the horses looked at me, smiling at my reaction to what they had found. I've been on this land for nearly two decades and never found this place of beauty. There was plenty of food for the kangaroos and wombats in this sacred hidden grove. And the horses were all shining with health. Stop worrying.

We continue feeding out, noticing that they don't need as much in summer as they did last winter. That there is hay despite widespread droughts and fires. And hay suppliers telling us it's hard to find. Don't worry. I relaxed. I trusted. I thanked the wild horses who are my friends and teachers. Bless them.

And then the rain came – a drenching, soaking in kind of rain that made the creek all that more healthy looking. Suddenly it was okay to shower, and wash and clean the kitchen and floors. Suddenly there was green.

There are many realities in this matrix called life. And one thing I learned through my training as a shamanic healing practitioner, was that the more in balance I was, the more whole I was, the more balanced my world was. In other words, the more I was Love, the more the world smiled.

Living with nature and animals not only helps connect with meaningful values but it helps us understand the deeper spiritual truths and how to play the game of life. My brumby herd says "Trust. We always know where to find an oasis." And so it is.

Billie Dean is an award-winning author (Secret Animal Business) and she runs A Place of Peace where 300 farm and other animals live in peace and safety. She is the founder of the Deep Peace Trust, a charity set up to help care for these animals and spread the vision of deep peace for all species. She is also an indie filmmaker and comic with Wild Pure Heart, a world-renowned animal telepath and founded Rainbow Fianna, her school for animal sensitives and Earthkeepers. To contact: www.billiedean.com, www.wildpureheart.com, www.deeppeacetrust.com

Chalk and Cheese

Drawing upon her own parenting experience, Rita Maher shares with us some tips on creating Harmony between opposites.

'As different as chalk and cheese.' We have all heard the saying before. We relate it to our children, our siblings and so many others around us, yet do we appreciate the gentle balance of chalk and cheese, the same balance that exists in yin and yang?

Take a good look at your children, and most people who have more than one will say that one is quiet, attentive, introverted, while the other is boisterous, adventurist and sanguine. Some will have one who is sporty while the other likes to keep their head in a book. Opposite in most ways. They can be arguing one minute and then they are best of friends in the blink of an eye, all along sending the parent into tailspins trying to figure out the right approach on raising them. What works for one will not work for the other, yet to give different styles of parenting can be seen as unfair and even have one child feeling the other is the favourite. So how can you find balance and harmony with chalk and cheese? And how can you transfer this learning so that your children understand how to communicate and respond to those around them who are different in personality?

Firstly, acknowledge that each child is a unique individual who cannot be placed in a hole that they don't fit. Just as you and your partner will respond differently to the way people speak and behave around them, it is only natural that so will your children. It is important to understand that while your children are different, neither one is better than the other. In fact the differences they possess, just like shadow and light, are often the very thing that allows for balance to be achieved in your home. It comes down to how you look at it and work with it.

Rather than seeing our children's differences as opposing, see them as complimentary.

Working out how your child thinks is a big part of creating harmony in the home. This is not a hard process. Take the time to observe and really get to know your child. Ask them about likes, dislikes, what makes them happy, sad, scared, or loved. They may surprise you. The way that you speak to them will have a big effect on the way they respond. You may find that you need to change and adapt your ways in order to gain the best results. Let's face it, if you have a child who is introverted, screaming at them to get them to do things will be like screaming at a brick wall. On the same note, if you have a child who is prone to outburst of screaming themselves, you will only add fuel to the fire if you start yelling. Take some time and trial different ways of working with your children. Think about how you would feel if your boss spoke to you in a bad way, and then think about how you would like to be spoken to. Sounds simple, yet we can forget this after long days at work and sleepless nights.

Play to their strengths and interests and help them develop in areas they may lack. The child who bounces off walls can benefit from outdoor activity. Encourage this, while involving your other children as well. Depending on their age, set up soccer or pole tennis games, get all of you on the trampoline and jump away some craziness. For the child who has their head forever in a book, encourage them to share the information or the story at dinner time. Whilst your other child may not like to read, being read to by their brother or sister can be great activity that allows for bonding. Encourage idea sharing and work towards common and individual goals, supporting each child as they achieve them. Set a family goal and encourage each person to contribute. Ask them how they think they can help if they are old enough.

Your children love you and love their family, yet can feel that at times the house may be too busy for them to be seen or heard, so make time. Set a date night with them. Yes you read right, set a date night. Make it fun - perhaps it's a game night, or getting your child in the kitchen to help you cook. How about homemade pizza and the children take the orders and create the meal together. Perhaps some one-on-one time with a parent, a Saturday afternoon with dad walking in the park. Create a hobby together that becomes a special time for you and your children.

When your children argue, use this time as an opportunity to understand the other's point of view. This is not a long drawn-out counselling session rather a quick "he likes this and you like that, what you said hurt because, how would you feel, let's make up and learn to comprise." Children don't want long-winded, drawn out explanations. They want to move past it quickly yet effectively. If there needs to be a punishment for bad behaviour, ensure it works for that child and fits the crime, and importantly be consistent.

Harmony and balance is something that we all strive for, not just in our family but our social and working lives. If we get this right now we can set strong foundations for our children to learn from. When they learn how to interact and appreciate each other's differences, then they are well-equipped for later life when they will meet and interact with many different people. So rather than look at chalk and cheese as two opposing forces, look at the beauty of the whole package working together.

Rita Maher is a Psychic Medium, Intuitive Counsellor and qualified Reiki Healer who has a passion for working with children and families. She specialises in meditation and intuitive guidance to help not just children but adults understand direction and change in their life, helping create secure environments for young minds to grow and thrive.

How to Relieve Stress and Get Back Your "Flow"

Meadow Linn gives a scrumptious way of Getting Back your Flow…

I nearly ran out of gas this morning. The orange light glared at me from the dashboard with its menacing, ominous glow. There's a gas station just a couple of blocks from my house, but I'd left my purse at a friend's home, and there wasn't enough fuel in my car to retrieve it. So, I ransacked my bedroom looking for cash, but apparently I'd already spent my "in case of emergency" stash. Then, I overcooked my eggs and tripped on the dog food.

I've been feeling a bit off-kilter for the past few days. The blues have come and gone like the ebbing and flowing of the tide. Rather than greeting the mornings with a grand ol' "Hooray! Welcome new day!" it's more of an "Oh no, another day."

I have a fair amount on my to-do list, but to be truthful, I've done a lot more with a lot less time in the past. But, stress doesn't always follow the laws of reason. An impending deadline can warrant a feeling of dread and despair one time and the next time, it's no big deal. Sometimes when faced with the exact same to-do list, I can feel as though everything is in the flow, and other times it's like swimming upstream.

Although it seems like the best way to relieve overload would be to buckle down and plough through the to-do list, I've found that I'm more productive when I feel good. Spending time being active outside seems to help the most, but I've also found that going to the gym, cleaning my house, and meeting a friend for a meal are all useful ways to get out of my head. In many ways, it's like hitting the "restart" button on my Mac.

This morning, for instance, after finally getting gas for my car, I went to the gym and then when I returned home, I spent an hour vacuuming the carpets, scrubbing the sinks, and making the beds. All the activity (plus the fact that my house was now clean!), made me feel better. Later, when I spilled a full cup of coffee on my white couch, it was no big deal. My flow was back. Spilling coffee may seem "out of the flow," but my reaction is what changed. And, to be honest, that's all that really matters.

Although there are myriad causes for feeling out-of-sorts, it can be valuable to ask yourself: "Am I stressed?" Often when I feel like the world is imploding around me and nothing seems to be going right, the root cause is stress. Once I acknowledge that my life doesn't actually suck; I'm just feeling overwhelmed, I can find a way to change my state. It might feel unproductive to take time away from your busy day, but when I'm in a good mood and feeling relaxed, I'm both more joyful and more productive.

"In the Flow" Apple Pancakes (Gluten- and Dairy-Free)

I was so "in the flow" when creating this recipe that the ingredients and quantities seemed to magically reveal themselves. For instance, although most pancake recipes call for only one egg, somehow intuitively I knew this recipe would need three. I didn't even need to tweak the recipe or do multiple test batches, these came out perfectly the first time!

- (Makes eight 4-inch pancakes)
- 2 tsp. lemon juice
- ½ tsp. baking powder
- ½ tsp. cinnamon
- 1 cup canned coconut milk
- 1 cup brown rice flour
- ¼ tsp. sea salt
- 2 Tbsp. coconut sugar (or brown sugar)
- 1 firmly packed cup of grated apple (from 1 apple, peeled and cored)
- 3 eggs
- Coconut oil for cooking the pancakes

- Using a liquid measuring cup, measure the coconut milk. Add the lemon juice and stir. Set aside.
- In a medium bowl, combine the brown rice flour, baking powder, coconut sugar, sea salt, and cinnamon.
- Peel and core the apple. Grate the apple using a box grater or food processor fitted with a grating disc. Add the apple to the flour mixture, and stir to combine.
- Whisk the eggs into the coconut milk. Combine coconut milk and egg mixture into the dry ingredients.
- Melt a bit of coconut oil in a medium-hot pan or griddle. Using a ladle or small cup, pour enough batter onto the griddle to make a four inch pancake. Cook until the bottom is golden brown and the top is covered in bubbles, flip and cook for a few minutes more on the other side. Repeat. Enjoy with maple syrup.

Meadow Linn is a writer and a chef, living in California with her dog, cats and chicken. She believes that living well and eating well should be tasty and fun. Meadow has just co-authored her first cookbook with Denise Linn which is available now through Amazon. **Contact Meadow at:** *www.meadowlinn.com and www.savortheday.com*

HEALTH & WELLBEING

inSPIRIT | review

RETURN TO SOUL

Published by Robyn Collins
AUTHORED BY ROBYN COLLINS

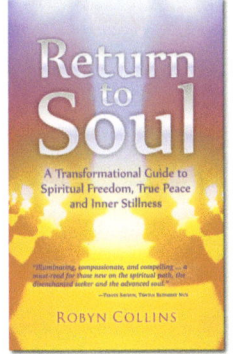

With a foundation in Meditation, Return to Soul provides you, the reader, with solid daily practices and routines to awaken your Spirituality and journey with your Soul to understand yourself to a greater capacity and on many levels.

Author Robyn Collins begins the book with bravely sharing her very personal journey of grief, searching, healing and awakening after the loss of her baby daughter. This opens the doorway for you to connect with the author as she shares her story in the hope that you too may find a ray of hope, some words of wisdom, or even find some peace in the knowing that you are not alone in difficult times.

With all the knowledge that Robyn gained through her own journey, part 2 of Return to Soul inspires one to align in their own integrity and authenticity, while using the exercises and tools provided to gain an understanding that spirituality truly is at the heart of the relationship you have with your own soul.

For any seeker of truth, Return to Soul is well worth considering adding to your library.

THE SECRET OF LIFE WELLNESS

Published by Rockpool Publishing
AUTHORED BY INNA SEGAL

Inna Segal's first book 'The Secret Language of Your Body' is a bedside table companion for myself and I refer to it often. I greatly anticipated reading this book and Inna truly has taken her work to the next level.

Based on 21 major questions Inna is constantly asked in her healing work, each section is abundant with explanations, real life stories, practical exercises and healings that are simple and can be life changing, that you can work with to be the owner of your healing journey.

Covering all aspects of human life that present challenges in some form, including developing intuition, relationships with love, family and friendships, pregnancy, home, attracting money and success, challenging emotions, soul mates, health, soul purpose, shadow side, grieving, energy centres to heal and evolve, and unconditional love, this book is a manual for self awareness, healing and living your best life.

COSMIC CODES CONT'D

The new moon in Gemini offers a welcome change as new and more playful energy flows in. We are encouraged to open our heart and mind, and try new ways of thinking and being. It's time to lighten the load and inject more fun and variety in to our daily life. Expressing ourselves openly, honestly and encouraging others is important now. Do your best not to rush or take on more than you can handle this month. It's time to stop and smell roses, connect with others and take notice of the important things in life.

June 2014

A month of opportunity and possibility with the full moon in Sagittarius on the 13th followed by a new moon in Cancer on the 27th. The full moon reminds us that we are all connected and what we do to ourselves directly affects another. Our words and actions need to be supportive, encouraging and come from a place of love and acceptance. Finding stillness within our daily life is essential this month as is the need to focus on our dreams and aspirations. It's a powerful time of manifestation, build it and it will come!

The new moon in Cancer is encouraging us to come out of hiding and be real about how we feel and what we sense. Children, family and relationships take centre stage and we are reminded to view our current situations from a fun-loving perspective. Setting emotional boundaries will be essential as we can be particularly sensitive and emotionally vulnerable at this time. Inner child work is especially favoured now.

Secret Animal Business
A Celebration of the Secrets of Animals, Their Forgotten Language and How They Can Help You and the Planet Heal

Billie Dean's award-winning book *Secret Animal Business* changes lives - the lives of the book's readers as well as their animals. Drawn from Billie's 30+ years as a professional interspecies telepath, the book is the ultimate handbook of enlightened animal care, with everything from diet to the world of energy to tips on how to communicate with them. It is chock full of heart-warming stories, and is a candid look into what it is like to grow up as an unltrasensitive.

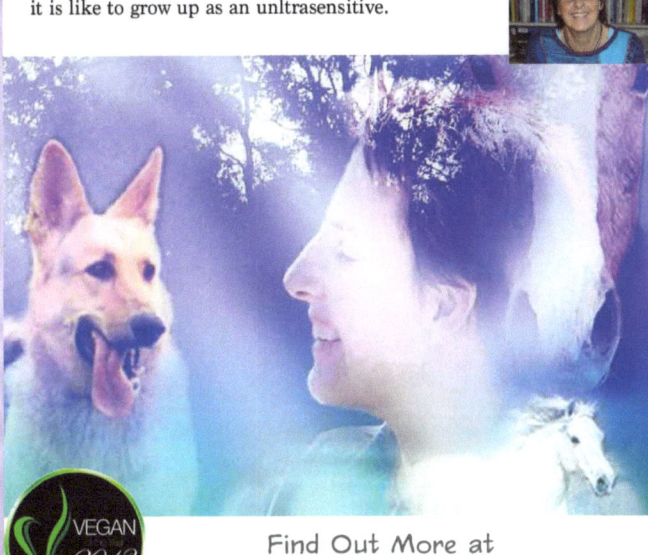

Find Out More at billiedean.com

inSPIRIT | Directory

ANIMAL SHAMANISM

BILLIE DEAN
Animal Shaman, Author, Teacher, Filmmaker
www.billiedean.com

ARTWORK

NICOLLE POLL
Artwork by Nicolle - Oracle Cards, Animal Magick Series, Soul Journey Portraits
E: artworkbynicolle@bigpond.com
FB: www.facebook.com/ArtworkByNicolle

NICOLA MCINTOSH
Graphic Design, Fairy & Fantasy Art, Oracle Cards & Writer
www.nicolamcintosh.com

ASTROLOGERS

DAVID WELLS
Teacher, Qabalist, Astrologer, Author & Past Life Therapist
www.davidwells.co.uk

CRYSTAL SHOPS

JOPO FENG SHUI & CRYSTALS
2 Revesby Road, Revesby NSW
T: +612 9785 0798

SPIRIT STONE
For crystals & new age supplies
www.spiritstone.com.au

MAGICAL TOOLS

NATASHA HEARD
Blessed Branches
www.blessedbranches.com

GEM~MER
Cryshell Magic
www.cryshellmagic.com.au

NUMEROLOGY

AMANDA COPPA
Crystal Healer, Numerology & Astrology
www.facebook.com/cosmiccodes

PERSONAL GROWTH

KYE CROW
Wunjo Crow – Sacred Clothing, Animal Sanctuary & Sacred Journey into the Animal Realm workshops
www.camelcampsanctuary.com
www.facebook.com/Wunjocrow

PSYCHICS & MEDIUMS

KERRIE WEARING
Author, Soul Coach & Medium
www.psychicmedium.com.au

Would you like your listing included here? Email us at
mail@inspiritpublishing.net for details.

SCIENCE & SPIRITUALITY

BRENDAN D. MURPHY
Author - The Grand Illusion
www.brendandmurphy.net

SHAMANISM

LAURA NAOMI
Consultations, Workshops & Seminars
www.laura-naomi.com

STORYTELLING & FOLKLORE

REILLY McCARRON
Faerie Bard, Folklorist & Storyteller with Harp
www.faeriebard.com
E: info@faeriebard.com
F: Faerie Bard

RADIO SHOWS

www.ghostsofoz.com

The Inaugural Australian Fairy Tale Society Conference

WHEN: Monday 9th June, 2014 (*the Queen's Birthday public holiday*).

WHERE: Paddington Uniting Church, 395 Oxford Street, Paddington, NSW.

PRICE: $95 standard / $80 AFTS member ($25 *AFTS annual membership*)

THEME: 'The Fairy Tale in Australia'.

The day will include academic papers, storytelling performance, readings, art exhibitions and a discussion panel. Morning and afternoon tea and a light lunch will be provided.

- Keynote speaker - *Carmel Bird*.

Contact: Reilly McCarron or Jo Henwood: http://www.faeriebard.com/afts/
- https://www.facebook.com/austfairytales • austfairytales@gmail.com

Advertise with Us

Advertise with inSpirit Magazine for :

- Best price value advertising,
- Your targeted market
- Cross promotion with Facebook and our email database

Contact us today at email: mail@inspiritpublishing.net

Volume 7 Issue 1
The Wholeness and Harmony Issue
www.inspiritmagazine.com

www.ingramcontent.com/pod-product-compliance
Lightning Source LLC
Chambersburg PA
CBHW041201290426
44109CB00002B/91